Journey

PITT POETRY SERIES

Ed Ochester, Editor

Journey

New and Selected Poems, 1969–1999

Kathleen Norris

University of Pittsburgh Press

Published by the University of Pittsburgh Press, Pittsburgh, Pa. 15261

Copyright © 2001, Kathleen Norris

Manufactured in the United States of America

Printed on acid-free paper

10 9 8 7 6 5 4 3 2 1

ISBN 0-8229-4137-6 (cloth)

ISBN 0-8229-5761-2 (paper)

The publication of this book is
supported by a grant from the
Pennsylvania Council on the Arts.

for David

Contents

Journey

A Prayer to Eve

Mother of fictions
and of irony,
help us to laugh.

Mother of science
and the critical method,
keep us humble.

Muse of listeners,
hope of interpreters,
inspire us to act.

Bless our metaphors,
that we might eat them.

Help us to know, Eve,
the one thing we must do.

Come with us, muse of exile,
mother of the road.

Poems 1969–1973

By night on my bed I sought him whom my soul loveth:
I sought him, but I found him not.
I will rise now, and go about the city in the streets,
and in the broad ways I will seek him whom my soul loveth,
    but I found him not.

—Song of Solomon, 3:1–2

Celebrations

The Window Box

Dampness
at my feet   what grows there
will smother me   I wish
I could bend down,
begin to feel the sides,
the shapes
of the sides
                and shadow, see
        what is in
the room and know
        what pulls at me
so
    gently, tending me
        carefully,
toward the light

Throb

You cut me
into pieces and
put them in separate corners
of the room
each part
placed under pillows
or into water

I grow from this darkness
like starfish
my fingers know the shape to take again

The Angel

L'ange avait replié ses ailes pour ressembler à tout le monde.
—"L'Ange," Louis Emié

When I died the first time
they made it so I could live   cutting under
my skin putting tubes
into my arms
and sides   my body fed
all day
and night pain seeped into my bones
my mouth had one infant syllable
for it all

I got up this morning   blue crickets
     in my eyes:
     blue, and
     in the mirror
     they shine
and the angel has hidden its wings
under the bed   its bejeweled wings
gather dust
under the bed,
my bones forget what they were, fox,
fish, or tree:
     all night I hung
     by my wrists
     in your room,
     waiting for this morning

Eating is so arbitrary

You fed me soup
and bread

Tomorrow

Tomorrow I said I would fly
six thousand miles and back
without eating but it's no use,
only angels travel light as that
and again this morning
I found myself
buried under thousands of shoes
on the closet floor.
There will be more of them
tomorrow, I will need the bags I packed
years ago, kept locked in the next room
all this time.

Tomorrow I said
you could see all the skin
I never showed
on the city streets,
but I think I can tell what will happen:
the explorer arrives by ambulance
instead of airplane,
and the bandages he brings along
are transparent, as useless
as memory

I wish I was like the sky is today,
so sure of itself:
it has no fear like this,
moving with suitcases
from place to place.

Falling Off

I thought it would happen someday:
easily, certainly,
with the aid of a miraculous cancer
or a needlessly spiteful lover

I expected some signal,
clear and unmistakable,
the horizon a place
where the edge was
and you had to watch your step

There is nothing now in sight
except the city, vertical
and bottomless,
where the worst things happen
and everything stays the same.
What year was it you said,
"You'll need a lot of tedium to get by"?
This present moment seems to be lasting forever

Running through Sleep

I would prefer to live quietly in silks,
like a lady, in a place where a lady lives,
but I have seen this body I carry around alone;
streamlined for sleep,
it is a fish swimming through dark water,
a fire burning undetected,
watching everything around it
turn to soft, wet ash.
It tries to recall the shape of a foot,
or a face smiling in a photograph,
something it can fit into
so it won't disappear.

Sometimes it is no more than dampness
on the underside of rocks,
running without a trace into the earth
and the roots of plants,
but at night the shoes of people
with the sweetest laughter,
the gentlest step,
are shoes with knives in the soles
that cut three feet deep,
and the heart seeks refuge
in the oldest, smoothest stones.

Sometimes it feels like the water forming in clouds,
commanding a view of continents,
and the ocean's edge;
but it fears falling from such a height
and having no place to go;
it fears that the police will find it rummaging
through someone else's closet,
stuffing its heart with rags.

Evaporation Poems

I would like to be as mobile as my mind
I had a religious aunt who was
(she flew out a window
into the Ideal).

So much noise:
the water in stems,
the workings of teeth,
intestines. Such
foolishness, she said,
wanting to be free
of breath's rise and fall,
wanting to be
no body.

2.

Transformation
has its price.
Do not dare to say that the water's need
is a simple one,
or that we shall all be changed.

3.

All summer I have watched the water
take whatever shape it can,
whispering "there is the past,
and the future, and between the two of them
you must be careful not to disappear."

Now I see so clearly on the days
when rain turns to snow,
how wind passes quickly
along the surfaces of things,
how calmly it probes this chilly place
where I have moved
with everything I own.

Stomach

My stomach is of many minds,
it believes everything it eats.
My eschatological
stomach, a fundamentalist
of sorts, grows intent
at drawing blood from
surfaces of things:
ice-cold fingers touch its inner lining,
it lives in fear of confusion.

The stomach clenched
its teeth, its nose bled all day
as I stumbled through snow,
cracking theories of poetry
over its skull.
Gilded toothpicks,
sweet-sour pork
did a desperate violence
to its body.
It had to be saved, put to sleep,
but it woke early,
still restless with envy of the resplendent
spleen.

I will be good to my stomach
tomorrow: listen, and believe it
for a while. The stomach
is serious and unhappy.
It wants to do something really
symbolic: it wants to be
the ultimate
stomach.

Eve Alone, in the Garden of Eden

It's easy to feel like a whore
in here.
Fishermen, potato farmers
go in and out
and the plumbing whistles all night.

The venetian blind falls down,
the kitchen drain backs up.
I pay for what I eat.

Female
generosity, that's what it is,
trouble every time,
and the goddamn plumbing whistles
all night.

Listening to Music Alone

Like the tree
no one hears falling, or,
as Emily put it,
sherry the guest
leaves in the glass.

Old photographs,
like good intentions,
the sound of a clock.
How it is
in here, how one night passes
through a needle's eye.

Extravagant music:
rain on asphalt,
a radiator's voice.
The refrigerator dances in a corner.

Blue Mountain

Do you understand?
You could point to things
like the lodgepole pine
and I was grateful:
nothing in the present tense
except a view, midsummer,
of that feathery tree.

When I left the Garden of Eden
my dress was wrong-side out.
Do you understand?
There are men I could spend eternity with,
but not this life.

Here in the city, it's not so bad.
I can picture the lake's edge
where you stand,
silent and indifferent;
the mountain behind,
the Angel at the gate.

Bean Song

A bean does not know much,
but it remembers the winter.
It sweats in secret, its skin grows tough
and smooth as it pushes up against the darkness,
against the weight of the universe.
Somehow it displaces just a little earth,
and everything shifts to one side.

The bean flower stands up
to see if it's in the middle of a field,
or someone's flower pot;
it is beautiful and bitter,
and dies after a while,
but the bean keeps singing to itself
a song about the stars,
and the cities, and the people
who live in sunlight.
No one hears it singing,
only a few ever learn the song.

At night, when I sleep alone,
I sing it for you.

Excerpts from the Angel Handbook

Be careful how you unfold your wings—
there are some in the world who are not content
unless their teeth are full of feathers

You may find employment with the Sanitation Department
or at any laundry

When you ride subways wear ornate silver shoes
and always stand near the door

When you cross at intersections look both ways, then up

It will often be expedient to altogether remove your wings
from your back, where people will first think to look for them,
and carry them around inside you—
at such times be careful that your hands do not forget
and begin to imitate their beating in your heart,
for if you begin to fly, the police will be called
and you will only confuse them

You will find that you are most free
when you are able to sit still

You will have a great fondness for music,
but be sure to hide your ears when listening to it,
for they will throb and grow

You must listen to what people say
even when they talk to you: this will involve
keeping silent much of the time, and being bored a lot

You will never tell a lie,
but you will have many secrets

At times it will seem that we have deserted you but
when people take you in, you will leave their teacups glowing,
their windows shining

You are not especially alert to danger but at times
you will sense an uncontrollable desire to warn others
of impending doom: to yell "Watch Out!"
as they stroll under low hanging branches,
or along the edges of pits

You will meet some who wear their faces nervously,
who will tell you how it seems
they will not survive.
These are the children; they still have parents,
or still need them

Many things you do will seem strange to them:
remember their savage origins,
be gentle and kind

As you find no situation intolerable,
they will think that you are cruel

Making decisions will be the most natural of tasks
but it will rarely seem necessary to make promises

Their logic will not make sense to you,
their mathematics especially will be impossible,
for you will never be able to divide anything

For amusement, look at the picture books:
angels there have huge white wings, silken robes,
long fine hair, and always look like eunuchs

You will meet some whose faces give a glow
as if they once had halos:
these are the lovers,
you will make a lot of love

and your flights, even though you are careful
to keep them invisible, will make those who love you sad:
they will not understand that you never go anyplace
you're not meant to be.

Space Walk/Self Portrait

the lightning and I had to pass together . . .
—Henri Michaux, *Miserable Miracle*

1.

The world is flat:
horizontals, equations,
people talking like machines,
buildings that look like people,
windows with the vacant fire
of a cat's eyes.
I want to die, so I can't sleep
I want to think, so I take a symbolic piss
This is not a space walk so much as a bathroom melodrama

2.

Late night
in the big city, and my neighbor the opera singer
is messing around on the scale of time.
The plane that took me and my lover above all this
crashed an hour ago
and there wasn't even a tree around
to repeat the word "forever."

3.

I step through a door
and the room becomes an empty canvas.
It's better to dream
than not to dream
in a room such as this,
where everything has been purified by loneliness.

I throw some tissues at the mirror, slowly,
one by one,
as if they were real flowers,
as if this were a real train, passing
through a small town
in the dark.

Kansas Anymore

Clouds roll over Manhattan
the way the earth settles
on the dead. Each circumstance—missing a bus,
buying a rug—comes to weigh something
in time. I roll the stone off my stomach
to get out of bed while soldiers overlook
the smallest happiness.
They wait for me on the street
and subway.

It's possible to fool them, to leave an innocent shoe
in New York City while dropping a red hat
over Kansas. It is possible
to make the most tender emotions
impervious to their bullets, arrows, and spears,
to become so purely
and invisibly present
that they will not think to look for me
as I walk beside them, or appear as a window
or door. Harboring a secret joy,
I move along bedroom walls
as they strap themselves
in sleep, afraid that death might pass through them,
and they would not know it.

They search for me,
but do not see. I become a trick
of light, the way a cat
keeps an immense space
within its eyes, and turns quickly to reveal it,
and turns away.

At a Window, New York City

When I drink
I'm the only one here:
a nun with baggage,
a scholar duck-walking,
a shard for archaeologists
above the Manhattan Fault.

An exile from Afghanistan
might find his mountains.
I look for silos
on the tops of buildings:
penthouse treebelts,
breaks of shadow.

When I drink I live alone,
a piece of skyline
going out
like ice and alcohol,
in the pattern of light.

Poems 1974–1981

The watchmen that go about the city found me: to whom I said,
Saw ye him whom my soul loveth?

It was but a little that I passed from them, but I found him whom
my soul loveth: I held him, and would not let him go, until I had
brought him into my mother's house, and into the chamber of
her that conceived me.

—Song of Solomon, 3:3–4

On the Northwest Hiawatha

Up the coast from Seattle, then east into mountains. A full moon.

Where there are mountains, there are rivers. Our sleeping car is "Skykomish River."

Sleep torn apart in the upper bunk. Forbidden territory. I remember that, and the Pullman being taken down, the fold-up toilet, and in the dining car, yellow flowers in a glass vase. A crisp tablecloth. There are children on this train, to remember other things. The people I traveled to see then are dead.

Near dawn. A man outside Paradise, Montana, carries a long metal rod through a field, balancing like a trapeze artist.

My husband is still sleeping. I go alone to the dining car. We stop in Missoula: two men are asleep in the yard, lying against a building. The bricks look old.

I read, without much interest, in the dome car. As we cross the Continental Divide, a man across the aisle says:
    "Of course, I've seen this before."
    "Three times," his wife adds.
"You know a fact when you see one, Archie," Nero Wolfe is saying, "but you have no feeling for phenomena."

My husband is half-dressed, looking out the window. "Are we still in Montana?" he asks, as we speed by the edges of towns. Frame houses sliced by noon-time shadow. Something is going on inside the houses: conversations, mysteries.

Night again, and I look for names of towns in the neon glare: John Deere, American Legion Post, A and W Root

Beer. I imagine lovers walking under trees. Streetlights give the trees a stage-show gaudiness that the lovers do not notice. I imagine a doctor and an undertaker, deep in talk, leaning on a bar.

Fires along a river. A string of fires. Men move in and out of the small red halos.

Even in the dark, one learns the land: farm lights far apart, the human fabric worn thin. We move closer to my grandmother's garden, rich with earthworms and manure, to the bed where my mother was born, where we will sleep, again, tomorrow.

Inheritance

Charlotte Totten, 1891–1973

1.

In the house are all her years:
linen dishtowels
ironed, starched, folded.
Fine wood:
bird's-eye, hard rock maple
which she oiled and rubbed.
I keep her powder jar,
and throw out her yellowed corsets
and white gloves.

I throw out the bottles of pills
for her heart, and small tins of rouge.
In the house is her King James:
pressed leaves,
prayers clipped from newspapers,
a photograph of a baby in a coffin.

The noon whistle blows.
I watch the minister
as he walks home to dinner.
Teach me, Lord,
to be gentle in all events, especially in disappointments;
let me put myself aside.

2.

In the kitchen, I put my own plants
by the window.
This is where jelly bags hung in summer
with crab apple, buffalo berry,
and she set table,

laying out a cloth,
filling each glass with water.

Her talk was of measuring, pouring, waiting.
This is where she made divinity and caramel
at Christmas.

3.

In June, 1917, men laid the sidewalk.
Children still skate on it
and learn to bicycle.

I keep her garden,
worrying for the spent columbine and daisy
that sleep through winter
in beds of straw.

The rain barrel stands
full of dark water, in the dark.
It opens its mouth as if to speak.

Cows

F. C. Totten, 1886–1973

My grandfather loved cows.
Raised them, ate them, spent their money.
Sunday drives past the ranch, when I was little,
he would point to a calf and say,
"See that one?
That's yours." I always believed.
I would stare out the back window
until my cow disappeared on the horizon.

The last time I saw him
he told me he used to get up in the cold,
before daylight.
I thought of this
as I fed him.
The cows must have seemed
the only warm thing, some mornings,
after his mother died.

"Don't divide the herd," he said
and over and over, the price per hundredweight
for God knows what year.
He didn't want to eat, because of the pain.
I asked him to talk to me about cows.

On the Land

Hills, a road
have obscured the land
where it was they lived:
now a blue space, a green space: nothing.

The thin path of a jet,
a hawk above a field.
There is no record
in all that air
of what they said to each other,
season upon season
of breeding and sorting cattle:
voices,
sharpnesses, angerings,
as they sat at table.

The kitchen flew out of her hands.

The river blazes, copper-colored, in the east.
The White Butte Road is a line, slate-blue.
To the west a man is riding.
She breathes in
the air, the distance,
and cannot move.

New Year's Eve in Bismarck, North Dakota

Flying in
before snow closed the airport,
waiting
for a way out,
drinking at the Patterson,
Peppermint Schnapps
for the season,
the town,
the storm.
The elderly bartender
wears a black
string tie.

A cowboy, drunk, says,
"You're lookin' good.
Got a figure like a bombshell.
Like an angel. An angel from outer space."
He leans in, close. "Some guys'd up 'n' say,
'C'mon, you're gonna have some.' I believe in God.
I'd never say that to a girl."

It's ten below
in Bismarck. They say it's colder
in outer space.
The Ecclesiastes
in my hotel room
is uncharacteristically hopeful.
"Better is the end of a thing,"
he says, loosening his loincloth,
"than the beginning thereof."

The Dancers

We are curious about one another's bodies
but courtly now,
assume the prescribed position:
your hand on my back,
our fingers meeting, holding in air.

We move where instinct moves us
on the stage-lit dance floor,
the strong farmer's son
and preacher's daughter
holding each other gingerly,
keeping distance, like possibility,
between us. I would like to feel your blonde head

between my legs, hear animals breathe
in the fields around us
as we get up, shivering,
and the moon steps down, still hungry,
in the pale grass.

The Middle of the World

The night is cloudy
a man with a lot on his mind,
a naked woman,
sit in the middle of a field, in the middle of the world.
It is quiet there.

He is like a horse,
making friendly gestures,
his body unexpectedly silky.
Shuddering, he reaches up inside her
rocking her
on the inland sea.

He shivers, half-clothed.
He'll work cattle tomorrow
if the weather holds.
She is naked, creamy.

They give back
the waters of the air,
and the moon, descending,
goes far into their night,
their faces and their lives:
this night, and the world, unfinished.

Calentures

A disease incident to sailors within the tropics,
characterized by delirium in which the patient, it
is said, fancies the sea to be green fields, and
desires to jump into it.

—*Oxford English Dictionary*

The fields appeared, running like old dogs
through our nights and days.
We ran them dog-faced,
not caring where the Pleiades lay,
or the North Star,
jeweled fields, where once we lay
in darkness, our loves around us.

They are gone
into the moon's arms,
white fields where grass is cut and stacked
against the winter,
and women labor in their beds:
blue and silver fields of wind
and deadly sun.
The smiling bride and groom are gone
into the moon's arms.

What I find
is wild mustard
and the green, hills
where foxes run or stand
in the cool grass.
They say it is a dream that passes,
a fever: I am out of place, they say.
Still I know
how it reduces:
riding in a thirst, bone-dry
in a heat,
these bitter fields.

A Place on Grand River

You took me once to your place on the Grand:
the first log house
your father made: the one-room stone,
the two-story frame.
They flooded out, except for the last,
built on higher ground.

You were the boy in the attic.
Your bed was still there, the patchwork quilt
half-rotten. You could still pick out
your first vest, and one of your mother's dresses.
I watched you rage through the rooms,
turning things over,
working like a thief, growing manic.

You pocketed a whetstone.
In the kitchen, china plates
were set
as if someone were returning.
You said: we sold it, up and left,
moved to town, bought plastic dishes.
What year was that? You didn't recall.
You were fourteen. Nineteen-sixty. Sixty-one.

We made our way in waist-high grass
to a ruin of cars, corn pickers,
tools. Things you could have used.
There'd been a buckboard. Antique collectors got the wheels.
There's no use now, you said.
We stood a while in the bitter loveliness:
cottonwoods, a turn of the river,
hard-won fields, abandoned. In big, swimming motions
we returned to where we'd come through the fence.

I know it seems a loss.
The ghosts are in things
you've had to steal back: your grandmother's cast-iron griddle,
your father's whetstone. My fields are mostly gone
to asphalt and tract houses.
Jim, we were lucky
other ways, on childhood's holy ground.
You got
animal timing, I got a way of saying things:
nothing is ever lost.

Getting Lucky

We've stopped running,
and hold each other carefully,
the brass bed floating,
a cloud of white and gold
in the borrowed room.

Just out the window
is my childhood Iowa;
hot narrow miles
to my father's church,
where the words of hymns
entered me
like dark wine.
Or is it yours:
the forested northeast,
where your German mother
sold dry goods, and your Indian grandfather
taught you to walk on moccasined feet,
feeling the earth's pull.

At Travis, during the war,
in that dead-silent terminal
where young men crossed over
or came home—some returned as freight—
we passed again:
you dutifully counting
bills of lading,
I a student,
full of books,
and a girlish impulse to save lives.

How dazzling you were
to the men returned from North Vietnam:
indelibly American

in a blue uniform,
clear-eyed, friendly,
a lesser angel
of account books,
missing years,
and back pay vouchers.

It's another year; we've traveled far.
Sunlight finds us
blessed with sleep,
the wine still heavy
on our tongues,
in a room beginning to feel like home.

The Year of Common Things

Just now a bird,
a sparrow,
landed on my knee,
your messenger.
The camp is well set. The weather's fine.
I sent fresh bread
so I could be a thought inside you.

On a green day such as this
we first went out
to sit by the river.
The lilacs had just come,
the late ice storm hadn't killed them
as we feared it might.
That would have been "the year without lilacs."
Instead, it was the year of common things:
lark buntings caught up in wind,
a dandelion flower as soft
as the inside of my wrist
which we did not pick
but left to open
into next year.

The bird's flown off. I close my eyes
to see your wind-burnt face,
our fingers meeting,
making a nest,
your head in my lap.

Harvest

We'll never belong.
The pheasant steps out of a medieval tapestry
into South Dakota,
this gravel road
is a thread the Fates cast down.
In 1897, my great-grandmother was buried
for twelve dollars and fifty cents.

I have the receipt,
some dress pieces, the strands of her hair
my grandfather kept hidden
for nearly eighty years.
He died then,
and I cut the sleeves of his long johns
to make a cover for my rolling pin.

His old truck
wheezes once and sputters forward.
The combine
spits out dust.
What will anyone
make of us? Two
childless
figures
in a field?

Dust

1.

She works among budding daisies, near a row of lettuce seedlings. She will seed the winter squash, and soon a cat will bring her a dead bird. Her husband will call her from the house and her body will tense with listening, then relax into laughter.

The windows are blue, still heavy with sleep. Outside it is already warm. She kneels in earth, pulling slowly. She wants to be touched: hands feeling her cheekbones and fine shoulders, her breasts. Kisses: gentle, or not very gentle. The sexual breeze began on a day such as this.

I will weed the columbines, she says to herself. There is much to be done.

The wind comes up suddenly, with great force. Intentions, mysteries: forgotten now. No one says: there were voices, a garden. Dust plays about.

2.

She gathers the last tomatoes. The cool sunlight is full of sound: rapids, a waterfall. It is only leaves, dry and rasping.

This was an ocean floor, and even now the air seems full of salt, full of waiting, and the land runs off in waves formed by the pulse of water.

It was a lake, where mastodons came to drink. A lakebed, a marsh. People came: walking, riding horses through the grass. Circles of fire, then homesteaders' fences, houses made of sod. They farmed recklessly. They planted trees.

It will be a desert.

3.

A man's white suit and a woman's dress are floating: ruffles of yellow, a silk rose on a lapel. They court now in the attic's dryness.

In the room below they lie in sheets patterned like waves in a Japanese woodcut, like nineteenth-century endpapers. They sleep in endpapers.

The clerk sets up in the kitchen. Faces crowd around a flatbed, fingering glassware, quilting pieces, picture frames, arrowheads, longjohns. The auctioneer begins to chant. Work gloves. Sold. For a dollar.

Light moves on the sleepers and on their house, gazing indifferently at the rose-colored rug. It moves, sure of itself, in the pattern made by a venetian blind. It strokes the books on a shelf, the reupholstered sofa, the unfinished afghan, as if to say: you too will settle, and be moved, for it is spring, or summer, or fall. Dust dances.

A cat scratches at the civilized pattern of an antimacassar: stops, looks around, resumes her task.

Photographs on a mirror: mother, father, daughter, son. No one names them now. The sleepers form words that are not spoken. Their hands touch lightly above their heads.

Washing Dishes Late at Night

The room tips
where we have rearranged it,
where lovers rode
as in a fairy tale:
now on a dragon,
now a horse.

The room cradles
their undressings,
their unencumbered arms and legs.
You dislodge them
with the new pictures.
I dip my hands in soapy water.

This was to be a poem about faith,
but the room tips uneasily
around our voices,
the pale light
in which we live, both of us afraid.

A Poem about Faith

My face is Mrs. Heyward's,
long and thin. In the photograph I have of her
she is sending a son
to the Great War. Her mother,
a mill owner's daughter from Manchester,
was disowned for running to America
with a Methodist.

I wear Mrs. Hutton's wedding ring:
it's washed countless dishes
at church suppers,
and pulled white shirts
through a steam-hot wringer.
I have her daughter's fine bones,
my grandmother Totten.
But I'll be stooped like grandmother Norris
when I am old, with alert eyes:
and while I may never have her faith in Jesus,
at the end, like her,
I know I'll expect to see my mother.

I have no photograph
of the milliner, a second cousin
who wed a doctor, against advice.
She ran away,
and police found her
in a far city, where she'd bought netting
and feathers,
but couldn't remember her name.

Or the girl raped at Bible Camp
by an old preacher, who spoke gently
as he lifted her skirts
and slid his hands

up her ten-year-old legs.
She sailed for Africa, and mission work,
when I was a child.

I have a scratched recording
of another aunt, singing hymns
in a rich soprano.
She heard the voices
of the lost tribes of Israel,
but her own voice led her
into temptation, and she seduced
a farm boy from the church choir.

She jumped out a window
at the State Hospital
the year I was born,
and I want more than anything
to know she has been forgiven.

Poems 1982–1986

I would lead thee, and bring thee into my mother's house, who
would instruct me: I would cause thee to drink of spiced wine of
the juice of the pomegranate.

—Song of Solomon, 8:2

For My Aunt Mary

1.

Mary, come home.
For too long you've wandered this prairie,
haunted by farm boys
with strong arms and big, sunburned faces.
We have nothing more to hide.

A photograph spoke to you
in the dust-bound parsonage,
the shaded room that held the past:
your aunt from West Virginia
modeling a hat
in her millinery store, not at all
proper
for a doctor's wife.
He sold the store;
she had a child
and ran away to Baltimore, where
she tried to smother the baby
in netting, felt, and feathers.

Her story possessed you
as a child. I heard your story
when I was twelve,
and wandered after
your bad endings,
thinking I'd never marry,
settling badly into it
when I did.
But my husband and I
made another story,
settled and more ordinary,
nothing a child might grasp
in darkness: your story ended then.

2.

Were you a Deborah,
called to battle? Or
a Magdalene, a witness?
You were just a small-town girl,
and no one would listen
or make room. You killed yourself
at the State Hospital
the year I was born,
a few days after you had your baby,
still Jesus' good girl, desperate
for God (diagnosis: "promiscuous,"
"talkative," "insight poor").

Even after you died,
the love went on consuming.
I know the hunger's terrible:
I love you, Mary,
I want to bring you rest. What you see
are the lovers in the garden,
before the Fall.
We both wish them well.
Come away from them now, Mary,
let them be.

Perennials

I've betrayed them all:
columbine and daisy,
iris, day-lily,
even the rain barrel
that spoke to me in a dream.

I inherited this garden,
and miss my grandmother
in her big sun hat.
My inexperienced hands
don't know what to hope for.

Still, flowers come: yellow,
pink, and blue. Preoccupied,
I let them go
until weeds produce spikes
and seeds around them.

I never used the rain barrel.
Water froze in the bottom;
too late, I set it on its side.

Now lily-of-the-valley comes
with its shy bloom,
choked by a weed
I don't know the name of. One day,
too late, I'll weed around them,
and pull some lilies by mistake.

Next year we'll all be back,
struggling.

Just look at these flowers
I've done nothing to deserve:
and still, they won't abandon me.

Pommes de Terre

Three women laugh aloud
in a sun-dappled kitchen
in 1927, in South Dakota.
They are learning French
to improve themselves.

Twice a week they come together:
today, they are naming vegetables,
"Haricots verts," one reads aloud,
pointing to the beans. "Green," says Elsa,
the German picture-bride,
lamenting the forests
she will never see again.
Lottie and Myrtle
recall a paradise of their own,
gentle hills at Sioux City, on down
along the river.

They laugh in the afternoon
in a house set down on a God-forsaken,
near-treeless plain.
Each tree they planted in town
either broke with ice
or wilted in the rainless summer.

"Chou-fleur," they say,
for cauliflower. Potatoes
are "pommes de terre."
The words have such a comforting sound
Lottie repeats them,
like a mother
comforting a child.

Oh, my little earth apples,
little "pommes de terre,"
my cabbage flowers,
oh yes: and now
the women's cheeks and breasts are blooming,
their bottoms grow round
in the chintz dresses.

They are ladies, yes,
pious and respectable,
but they are laughing now,
beyond caring.

Such elegant potatoes:
pommes de terre, my dear,
oh my dears, oh yes.

Housecleaning

The dreamer descends through the basement to
see what was valuable in her inheritance.
—Nor Hall, *The Moon and the Virgin*

Kneeling in the dust, I recall
the church in Enna, Sicily,
where Ceres and Proserpine reigned
until a Pope kicked them out
in the mid-nineteenth century.

This is my Hades, where I find
what the house has eaten.
> *And Jessica was left with only
> the raw, sheer, endless terror
> of being alone in the world.*
"We are alone, Jessica," I say aloud:
the whole box of romances must go.

I keep the photograph of a young girl
reading cross-legged
under cottonwoods,
her belly still flat, not yet a fruit
split open, the child shining
in its membrane
like a pomegranate seed.

She ended both their lives,
and no mother's rage or weeping
could bring them back.
I leave her with the book of fairy tales:
still safe, held fast
in Sleeping Beauty's bramble forest.

I could use some sleep.
What I do must be done

each day, in every season,
like liturgy. I pray
to Mary Magdalene, who kept seven demons,
one for each day of the week.
How practical; how womanly.

My barren black cat rubs against my legs.
I think of the barren women
exhorted by the Good Book
to break into song:
we should sing, dear cat,
for the children who will come in our old age.
The cat doesn't laugh,
but I do. She rolls in dust
as I finish sweeping.

I empty the washer
and gather what I need for the return:
the basket of wet clothes
and bag of clothespins,
a worn, spring jacket in need of mending.
Then I head upstairs, singing an old hymn.

The Wedding at the Courthouse

I don't like weddings.
When you live here long enough
the spindly-legged girls
grow up like weeds
to be mowed down: matrons
at twenty-five, all edges taken off.
When the music starts
they're led down the aisle
in their white dresses
and we celebrate sentiment
and money.

There's only one wedding
I'd go to again.
I happened to be on an errand
at the county courthouse
and Lucille came running:
"Will you be a witness?
We need two,
and the girls can't leave their desks."

They'd shown up
that morning, no family or friends.
Not kids: he looked about thirty
and she just a little younger.
She may have been pregnant,
but you couldn't tell.
It might have been the denim jumper
she was wearing.

I can picture Lucille
chain-smoking, surprised
and pleased
to interrupt routine.
And the Deputy Sheriff,
a young man, blushing,
loaded gun in his holster,
arms hanging loose.
He looked at his shoes.

It's the words I remember most.
Lucille put out a cigarette
and began: "Dearly beloved,"
and we were!

Young Lovers with Pizza

The curve of a smile,
of buttocks,
clothes everywhere,
pizza in a box, laughter
when the telephone intrudes
and you must untangle
legs, breasts, hips
to answer it.
It becomes
a private joke:
the person on the other end
doesn't know a thing.

I envy you,
couples in this town,
in the world:
that first touch, growing,
the dry, breathy heat
and kisses like cool water,
couples lost for a moment
inside each other, inside out.

Don't think of me,
or your duty to God
and telephone. This is silence,
holy and lucky:
a man's hard body,
skin soft to the touch, the giddy
generosity
of a woman's breasts,
as light curves gently
around the spinning earth,
around your smiles and
naked hips, holding
everything you need.

Eve of St. Agnes in the High School Gym

The saint's been dead too long:
no young girl keeps her vigil. Not one fasts
or prays tonight for a vision
of the man she'll marry.

A band plays—too loudly—
popular tunes a few years out of date.
Young men emerge from a huddle
of teammates, cheerleaders,
fans. They run onto the court,
howling, slapping hands.

Men just a few years older
stand smoking by the door;
their windbreakers advertise a local bar.
Others sit in the stands
holding sleepy children;
the women with them look worried and tired.

Snow falls silently,
snaking through the streets,
while in the gym, done up like spring
in a pale yellow skirt
and lavender sweater,
a pretty girl sleepwalks
on high heels. She carries herself
to a boy on the bench
who doesn't look up; and the old men sigh.

When the game is over
they flee on the storm.
The saint sits in heaven,
and if anyone's praying
on this chilly night,
let it be for love.

The Blue Light

1.

The angels stood
with their backs to me.
I was six months old
and dying.
I had no name for them,
for anything.
They were cold,
not like my mother.

Just beyond the angels
was a blue light
and like any child
I reached for it
because it was pretty.
I wanted to curl my fingers around it
and hold on.

The angels didn't move,
but the blue light receded.
Children are easily disappointed,
and I wanted it so much.

I lay in the hospital crib, angry,
rolling my head and crying. It may have been one of the angels
who picked me up
and returned me to my mother;
I don't know. But I knew my parents
were as helpless as I.

I learned it too soon.

2.

I learned to keep moving,
back through the pain.
I had no name for it.

And the nurse who fed me a bottle
through the operation,
the doctors working helplessly
with all their skill;
it was their world
I learned to want.

The love that moved me then
still moves me. I saw the perfect
backs of angels
singed with light:

I turned from them,
I let them go.

Numbers

I watched them chase each other
across the page,
the 1 grimacing into a 2,
and then a 3;
the 6 bouncing a ball up
to the 7,
the 7 bouncing it back.
The 8 skated elegantly,
entirely self-absorbed.

When the 1 married the 0
and became a 10,
I thought I'd had a glimpse
of heaven,
though I supposed the 9 was jealous.

I wanted to leave the numbers alone,
and let them have their stories.
But we learned to add,
and take away, and Sister said
that 2 plus 2
was always 4.

I knew this could not be,
but I liked her,
and pretended for her sake.

Dividing was hard,
and it always seemed we lost something:
a fraction would trail away
forever, vaguely accusing,
like an unbaptized baby
on its way to Limbo.

Multiplying
was the worst of all,
as glorious and impossible
as angels dancing in the playground.

I couldn't hold the numbers
in my head anymore; they'd become too big
and strange, standing off
to the side where
I couldn't see them,
even as they reached into my life.

Faith is a sad business.

The Age of Reason

> When I was four, I could draw as well as
> Raphael. It has taken me my whole life to learn
> to draw like a four-year-old child.
> —Pablo Picasso

1.

Late one summer evening
we thought you lost
in the ravine
behind the house. You told me once
God cut it in the earth, angry
because people would not love him.

You had built a cocoon of branches
and were curled
inside it, sound asleep.
We broke it open, unfolded you,
and carried you into the house.

After first communion,
I held the veil you handed me
and felt suddenly ashamed
that we'd broken in like that,
the branches too thick,
the entrance too low and narrow
for us to crawl through. And now
you'd seen us
for the fools we were,
celebrating nothing
in a disastrous place.

2.

Now it begins: the search for a God
who has moved on, the
God-please-help-me need
you still can't imagine, strangely
twisted landscapes
in which you may not rest.
The pillar of cloud
you saw march across the plain
will pass you by; some younger child
will see it.

It was given
so readily, and now you must learn
to ask for it back.
It's not so terrible;
it's like the piano lessons you love
and hate. You know how you want
the music to sound,
but have to practice, half in tears,
without much hope.

Little Girls in Church

I've made friends
with a five-year-old
Presbyterian. She tugs at her lace collar,
I sympathize. We're both bored.
I give her a pencil;
she draws the moon,
grass, stars,
and I name them for her,
printing in large letters.
The church bulletin
begins to fill.
Carefully, she prints her name—KATHY—
and hands it back.

Just last week,
in New York City, the Orthodox liturgy
was typically intimate,
casual. An old woman greeted the icons
one by one,
and fell asleep
during the Great Litany.
People went in and out
to smoke cigarettes and chat on the steps.

A girl with long brown braids
was led to the icons
by her mother. They kissed each one,
and the girl made a confession
to the youngest priest. I longed to hear it,
to know her name.

2.

I worry for the girls.
I once had braids,
and wore lace that made me suffer.
I had not yet done the things
that would need forgiving.
Church was for singing, and so I sang.
I received a Bible, stars
for all the verses;
I turned and ran.

The music brought me back
from time to time,
singing hymns
in the great breathing body
of a congregation.
And once in Paris, as
I stepped into Notre Dame
to get out of the rain,
the organist began to play:
I stood rooted to the spot,
looked up, and believed.

It didn't last.
Dear girls, my friends,
may you find great love
within you, starlike
and wild, as wide as grass,
solemn as the moon.
I will pray for you, if I can.

The Gift of Tears

You will be sitting with children
in the school gym,
watching dancers perform.

One will move out of view,
behind the lunch tables set on end
to make wings, a stage.
Soon only her feet will be visible,
flexing in black leg warmers,
like the feet of the Wicked Witch of the East
when Dorothy's farmhouse lands on her.

And in the middle of the night
when the tears come,
it will be because you married
after all, and moved West,
to a place where tornadoes take people up
in a mad embrace.

"These tears are all I have," I write,
and the next day I show the children
the page I scrawled in the dark,
and read the new poem I wrote
in their dull prairie town.
"Do you see how it works?" I ask,
and they nod, unsure.

"Do you live in a country?"
a little girl asks.
I don't know how to tell her.

It's our secret country,
where evil spells are broken
by a promise of love,

and little girls can melt away
the wickedness that's in them.

How I Came to Drink My Grandmother's Piano

It has to do with giving,
and with letting go,
with how the earth rotates
on its axis
to make an oblate spheroid.

It has to do
with how it all comes 'round.

There was a piano
in my grandmother's house.
I inherited it,
but never learned to play.
I used it as a bookshelf
and dust collector
and finally gave it to a church up the street.

I was snowed in at a trailer house
in Regent, North Dakota,
when Rita offered me a glass
of dandelion wine.
"That's some glass," I said,
much too fancy for our thrown-together meal
of hamburgers and fried potatoes.
"Yes, isn't it?" she replied,
fingering the cut glass pattern.
"A friend gave it to me.
Someone had given it to her,
but she never used it."

I began to hear that piano
as Rita poured the wine.
The dandelions spun around:
glad to be yellow again,
glad to be free of the dark.

The Monastery Orchard in Early Spring

God's cows are in the fields,
safely grazing. I can see them
through bare branches,
through the steady rain.
Fir trees seem ashamed
and tired, bending under winter coats.

I, too, want to be light enough
for this day: throw off impediments,
push like a tulip
through a muddy smear of snow,

I want to take the rain to heart
and feel it move
like possibility, the idea
of change, through things
seen and unseen,
forces, principalities, powers.

Newton named the force that pulls the apple
and the moon with it,
toward the center of the earth.
Augustine found a desire as strong: to steal,
to possess, then throw away.
Encounter with fruit is dangerous:
the pear's womanly shape forever mocked him.

A man and a woman are talking.
Rain moves down and
branches lift up
to learn again
how to hold their fill of green
and blossom, and bear each fruit to glory,
letting it fall.

Land of the Living

Menstruation is primitive,
no getting around that fact, as
I wipe my blood from the floor
at 3 A.M. in the monastery guest room,
alone in this community
of sleeping men.

Once again, I have given up
the having of children,
and celebrate instead
a monthly flowering
of the not-to-be,
and let it go without regret.

Earlier tonight, a young monk, laughing,
splashed my face
with holy water. Then, just as unexpectedly,
he flew down a banister, and
for one millisecond
was an angel—robed,
without feet—
all irrepressible joy
and good news.

The black madonna watched us,
expectant as earth just plowed.

My sister holds her baby
in a photograph. They smile at me
from the mirror I've placed them on.
Lili sits like the Christ child
on her mother's lap. She sits very straight
in a blood-red dress
and stares into something
that makes her look amused, and wise.

It's here, in the land of the living
the psalm says we shall see God's goodness.
I'm glad to be here,
a useless woman,
sleepless and kept waiting
as breath keeps coming,
as the blood flows.

A Letter to Paul Carroll, Who Said I Must Become a Catholic so That I Can Pray for Him

It's here, in the silent monastery corridor,
I think of you and say a prayer
for those lost by the way,
for the foolish virgins,
not the wise. It's your prayer, too, Paul,
for the losers
of eternal life, the unfaithful
departed, who sit alone
in the near-dark, writing,
Why—do they shut Me out of Heaven?

You and I know that now
Miss Dickinson descends a staircase
in the Elysian Fields. With her is
Miss Thérèse of Lisieux,
who said to Jesus,
I am happy not enjoying the sight of that beautiful heaven
here on earth, as long as you open it in eternity
for unbelievers. Here, Paul, where they pray
and cross themselves
and tend bees and run a print shop
and farm and come to choir
stinking of sweat. They're Catholic enough
even for you, and their prayers rise like incense
carried by the angels up to God.
Of course I believe it. Even the Methodist
in me believes in the change,
the bread and wine that turns into Benedictines
dressed like ravens
who reappear each morning
to pray and sing.

Of course I don't belong.
In habits as black as unbelief, as black
as the Black Madonna,
who answers all prayers from the heart,
they take me in out of charity.

When I'm among them
I say all the "Glorias"
and "Alleluias" and "Amens,"
and often I really mean it.
I don't know what I'm saying,
Paul, and that's the point.

"The Sky Is Full of Blue and Full of the Mind of God,"

a girl wrote once,
in winter, in a school
at Minot Air Force Base.
A girl tall for her age,
with cornrows and a shy, gap-toothed smile.
She was lonely in North Dakota,
for God, for trees,
warm weather, the soft cadences of Louisiana.
I think of her
as the sky stretches tight all around.

I'm at the Conoco on I-94, waiting for the eastbound bus.
Mass is not over; the towers of the monastery
give no sign
that deep in the church
men in robes and chasubles
are playing at a serious game.

I feel like dancing on this
wooden porch: "Gotta get to you, baby,
been runnin' all over town."
The jukebox is wired to be heard outside
and I dance to keep warm,
my breath carried white on the breeze.

The sky stretches tight, a mandorla of cloud
around the sun. And now
Roy Orbison reaches for the stratosphere:
something about a blue angel.
It is the Sanctus; I know it; I'm ready.

The Wine

for David

1

If you knew how they bored me,
dear, you'd never regret
not being one of my grand passions.

If you knew how cold
was that attention I gave them,
chilled to perfection, like champagne:

how we exhausted ourselves
and grew irritable
or worse,
as it all went flat.

2.

We set up battered lawn chairs
on the apartment roof
and sat down to see
how the sun went on.
Across the way a child played at sweeping
while a woman pulled laundry
off a line. It was New York City,
but the air seemed full of spices,
more like Jerusalem
than any town I knew:
the pale red roofs
of the East Village
turning gold,
then blue.

A few stars ventured forth,
a crescent moon between two tenements,

as stars made of wine
exploded on our tongues:
Dominicans and Methodists
singing in the corridors of childhood,
more solemn, in memory,
more in tune.

"We were all once
inside a star," you said,
the ever-faithful scientist.
The noise of the city was as constant as the sea.

3.

Fifteen years, driving through another country,
a sea-like prairie and a sky so full
I know that everything has changed,
you say, "We're looking at the center . . .
we usually see only the stars
on the end of our spiral wing . . . you know,
the Milky Way has two spirals,
kind of like wings . . ."

. . . Like an angel, I am thinking
as we head into the cloud of stars
at the center of our galaxy,
speaking of distant cities
and homemade wine. "All right,"
I say, "I love you."

The Astronomy of Love

"Would you like to see Venus?"
the old monk asks three women,
leaning out from his observatory
on a bright spring morning.
Gifts are the currency here:
we offer him the wildflowers we've picked,
and yes,
to see Venus would be good indeed.

"Imagine being weightless
as an angel," he says,
stirring his beloved science
with mystery, like water
into wine, the spin
the same as our own,
around Galactic Central Point.

"Timeless, too," he adds,
shaking his white head.
"There's no getting
from one place to another,
no getting at all." Retreating into silence,
he looks up his coordinates,
adjusts the azimuth, and hones in.

As much as he loves it,
he longs to throw the telescope away
and see the place where angels
and numbers are one. Meanwhile,
in the dark, old-fashioned sanctuary,
three corny angels ride their clouds
like goddesses, like Rita Hayworth
in 1948. Mary is at the center,

her womb a constellation.
In the wine cellar
blind Pérignon discovers his mistake,
a bottle left to ferment
for a second time. "I am drinking stars,"
was how he put it:
he wasn't kidding.

Why the Image of a Starry Womb
Is Not Poetic Claptrap but Good Science

Once,
in a fit of romance,
I wrote of a woman:
"She wants to break, but not end,
to hold him through the night
and like all lovers,
become not salt or tears,
but stars."

I threw it out;
it sounded too poetic.

Then I saw
the pregnant Virgin
contained in a rush
of seraphim wings, her blue mandorla
shot through
with starlight, shadow,
and a sober
quantum physicist
whispered in my ear, "each atom in your body
was once inside a star . . . "

I found the future
cradled
in this past:

called forth from stars
God calls by name—
this God who labors to give us birth—

we come,
as all things come,
to light.

Taking the Blue

Trees gossip
in the ghost-light. Early stars
climb the sky
and a breeze descends,
touching my arm
lightly, like my grandmother
at the last. I climb the hill
at the edge of town as
dust devils rise in the fields.

What is it for, any of it,
choosing to live
day in, day out,
in a parched land?

My grandmother's prayer, *Keep me friendly*
to myself, has weathered badly
in the long crescendo
of Romans 8. Her handwriting fades
on the yellowed page and I have failed to love
the river in the tree,
the stream in the grass,
the ocean of blood
that moves in us. I am,
inexplicably, here
and now, already taking
the next breath.

Trees gossip, and dark moves
like the ocean this land
once was: stubble, grass, ground,
turning in the last light
gold, green, blue.

Poems 1987–1999

Set me as a seal upon thine heart, as a seal upon thine arm: for
love is strong as death, jealousy cruel as the grave . . .

—Song of Solomon, 8:6

Cinderella in Kalamazoo

—The Medieval Institute, 1990

Unaccustomed to rain, hills,
trees overhead
gentle as a lover's hands,
I pass the student center where
medievalists crowd the cash bar,
pause on the steep path
to the dorm, remove my shoes
and am carried for a time
on waters deep as liturgy,
rain sifting through trees
like unexplained tears.
Compline has ended: Cistercians observing
Bernard of Clairvaux's nine-hundredth year
sang the "Salve Regina"
to a perfect, oceanic stillness.

Six-foot-two
and built like a barrel,
the hem of his habit rolling
like waves onto shore, my unlikely fairy godmother
bade me sing. "This is not
a spectator sport," he boomed, inviting me
to learn the chant. And as I joined the others
on the wild green ride
our song became conveyance,
a glorious means of passage
along a narrow road.

"Can you help me?" asks a monk at the door.
Midnight strikes
as we move a table into place
for morning Mass. I'll be gone by then, on a flight
to the known world,

through two time zones, my shoes
still soggy, to a drought-stricken plain:
back to my life, the man I love.

I will find it changed,
a dusty old house
where doors no longer fit their frames.

Giveaway

In the desert
dryness promotes the formation
of flower buds. This is not aesthetics,
but survival.

In the cancer ward, we laugh.
Solemnly attentive as a deacon
at Mass, a nurse prepares an enema.

Serena tells stories: Mrs. Long-Nose,
a childhood invention,
who moved by farting
in her voluminous skirts. The nurse laughs, too.

2.

There is flame
at the center,
gold center
of each bud.
Sometimes we see it,
when blooms are spent.

For three nights I have been sleeping
in Serena's star quilt,
wrapped in a daughter's song of needle and thread,
a song the color of parched grass.

3.

Joy at the heart of things:
Serena in the home, sightless at last,
asks to sit by the window
so she can watch the moon rise.

Serena with her daughter,
spending the last money
on bingo, and blankets for the funeral giveaway.

"Did you have fun?" a nurse asked.
"As much fun as you can have," Serena replied,
"playing bingo when you're blind."

Ascension

> Why do you stand looking up toward heaven?
> —Acts 1:11

It wasn't just wind chasing
thin, gunmetal clouds
across a loud sky;
it wasn't the feeling that one might ascend
on that excited air,
rising like a trumpet note,

and it wasn't just my sister's water breaking,
her crying out,
the downward draw of blood and bone . . .

It was all of that,
mud and new grass
pushing up through melting snow,
the lilac in bud by my front door
bent low
by last week's ice storm.

Now the new mother, that leaky vessel,
begins to nurse her child,
beginning the long good-bye.

The Ignominy of the Living

Elizabeth Kray, 1916–1987

The undertaker had placed pink netting
around your face; I removed it
and gave you a small bouquet, encumbering you
into eternity. "Impedimenta," I hear you say,
scornfully, the way you said it at Penn Station
when we struggled to put your bag onto a contraption
of cords and wheels. "Laurel and Hardy got paid for this,"
I said, the third time it fell off,
narrowly missing my foot.

You would have laughed
at the place we brought you to,
the hush of carpet,
violins sliding through "The Way We Were."
"Please turn the music off," I said, civilly,
to the undertaker's assistant.
We had an open grave—no artificial turf—
and your friends lowered you into the ground.

Once you dreamed your mother sweeping
an earthen floor
in a dark, low-ceilinged room.
I see her now. I, too, want to run.
And "the ignominy of the living,"
words you nearly spat out
when one of your beloved dead
was ill-remembered: I thought of that
as I removed the netting.

Today I passed St. Mary's
as the Angelus sounded.
You would have liked that,
the ancient practice

in a prairie town not a hundred years old,
the world careering disastrously toward the twenty-first century.
Then a recording of "My Way" came scratching out
on the electronic carillon.
"Oh, hell," I said,
and prayed for Frank Sinatra, too.

Epiphany

—Vladimir Ussachevsky, 1911–1990

The night you died
you rushed into the apartment
where I was sorting your papers,
weary as the girl
who has until sunrise
to spin straw into gold.
In a disreputable black raincoat,
well-traveled,
you were your old-world,
courtly self,
despite the haste, the fuss
of leaving.

From deep in your pockets
you drew out coins, ticket stubs,
a black-and-white photograph
of the Orthodox church in Manchuria
where you first learned liturgy, the ebb and flow
of choirs. More than sixty years
have passed: your first friends
on earth, dogs and birds
and tumbleweeds from the fields around Hailar
run silent as shadows through Calvary Hospice
in the Bronx, time and space
unraveling, dark threads at your hem.

Now my sister's baby wakes
in Honolulu, weaving his hands in air.
He hears the birds
and answers them,
calling to the light.

A. J.'s Passage

Poor baby, hold on;
poor, sleepy baby, passed into my arms.
We are passing through hell; hold on.
We renounce the forces of evil
and you cry out.

Poor, sleepy baby
wanting nothing more than the food
your mother has become
for you, wanting to go into
this night at her breast.

Brilliance
catches your eye,
the candle
in your mother's hand, her hair
a halo, your fingers transparent.

Poor baby, our words wash over you,
and you brush them away.
You want the candle now,
and you want your mother.
It is not yet time
to follow her into the dark.

Poor little baby,
water on your hair,
chrism on your forehead,
dried milk on your chin.
Poor brave little baby; hold on.

Mysteries of the Incarnation

1.

She Said Yeah

The land lies open: summer fallow, hayfield, pasture. Folds of cloud mirror buttes knife-edged in shadow. One monk smears honey on his toast, another peels an orange.

A bell rings three times, the Angelus, bringing to mind Gabriel and Mary. "She said yeah," the Rolling Stones sing from a car on the interstate, "She said yeah." And the bells pick it up now, saying it to Mechtild the barn cat, pregnant again; to Ephrem's bluebirds down the draw; to the grazing cattle and the monks (virgins, some of them) eating silently before the sexy tongue of a hibiscus blossom at their refectory window. "She said yeah." And then the angel left her.

2.

Imperatives

Look at the birds
Consider the lilies
Drink ye all of it

Ask
Seek
Knock
Enter by the narrow gate

Do not be anxious
Judge not; do not give dogs what is holy

Go: be it done for you
Do not be afraid
Maiden, arise
Young man, I say, arise

Stretch out your hand
Stand up, be still
Rise, let us be going . . .

Love
Forgive
Remember me

3.

True Love

binds all wounds,
wounds all heels,
whatever. You can tell.
William Buckley,
Gore Vidal, Samson
and Delilah. Paul
and the Corinthians.
You can tell.

It makes us fight
and bleed, takes us to the heights,
the deeps, where we don't
want to go. Adam and Eve, Noah
and Mrs., David,
Bathsheba, Ruth,
Naomi, Martha
and Mary. You can tell.

The way light surges
out of nothing. The Magdalene,
the gardener. God help us,
we are God's chosen now.

Luke 14: A Commentary

He is there, like Clouseau,
at the odd moment, climbing
out of the fish pond
into which he has spectacularly
fallen, announcing
to his hosts, the owners
of the estate: "I fail
where others succeed!"

You know
this is truth. You know
he'll solve the mystery,
unprepossessing
to the last, the last
of the great detectives.
He'll watch, and blend into the scenery
and more than once, be taken
for the gardener. "Come,

now," he says, taking us
for all we're worth: "Sit
in the lowly place."
Why not, we ask, so easy
to fall for a man
who makes us laugh. "Invite those
you do not know." He puts
us on, we put him on: another
of his jokes.

Return of Swamp Thing

> Keep awake . . . for you do not know at what
> hour your Lord is coming.
> —Matthew 24: 42

Watching the green man emerge from his swamp
in search of love,
I make popcorn and settle in
until Swamp Thing—one of the good guys—finds his gal,
a California blonde with creamy breasts
and bright blue eyes: an inspiring story,
except that she can't act.

It doesn't matter. At five, listening for the Jesus
who roams in the night,
I wouldn't let him take my party,
the juice and cookies
with the Easter bunny
at a department store in Washington, D.C.
I have the photo: me
with the bunny,
and Jesus; who knows?
He can have the TV set, maybe even
my popcorn maker. He can dress
in vines and carry me through the swamp
as the movie ends—
a what-the-hell
Hollywood smile
a flash
of those baby blues
as empty as the things
she thought she needed—and off she goes,
with Swamp Thing.

Is this the ending,
or did it just begin? Half-awake,

I listen to the wind brush snow
against the door. Any minute my husband
will enter, returning
from a long journey. I need to hear
that love wins out: even if
the girl's a dip,
and the actor, itchy
by the sixth retake,
flubs his lines: "That woman!" he cries,
"if I have to go
and save her one more time,
it's gonna kill me!"

It's the old impasse:
I don't know what to wait for.

Three Wisdom Poems

1.

LaVonne's Mantlepiece

"Did you know," LaVonne says,
"that schools are teaching Communism,
and not our American way?"
Remember now, LaVonne's a gentle person,
this is her way of making conversation
in a world full of danger: one sister
a Unitarian, another marrying
a Catholic. "It breaks my heart," she says,
fingering their photographs
on her mantlepiece.
Tonight she wants me to come with her
to a Church of God revival meeting.
"Do I look like I need reviving?" I ask,
and she laughs. But then
she gets her confused look,
and I remember that for all the abuse
LaVonne has taken in her life,
she's the least resentful person I know.
I say, "I guess all these churches
are doing the best they can,"
and LaVonne beams back: "Oh,
don't you think the true church is in the heart?"

2.

Physics Defeats Me Once Again,
But Wisdom Saves the Day

My sailor friend,
a useful man named Pete,
took me to meet her in a waterfront bar.

We sat in darkness,
away from the neon horseshoe
and I must have looked as stern
as a schoolmarm, for she stood there stark naked
and winked and called out,
"Smile, honey, this is serious."
"Yes," I replied, "I know."

For her finale,
she rotated her breasts
in opposite directions.
"I've always wanted to do that," I told her
when she joined us for a drink.
She looked at me appraisingly.

"You're too small," she said.
But she said it kindly,
and that's what matters.

My Favorite Woman in the World

The dogwood by the poisoned Susquehanna
is like some women
in love. Breathing in soot,
drinking water as brown
and stinky as shoe polish,
it gives back all it can
of blossom, and heavy with that grace,
bows low before the industrial gods of Harrisburg,
men who know how things are done.

My favorite woman in the world
died sometime in the fifth century.
She loved her husband,
the way some women will,
and built him a monument at Salonae.
Men had told her
how the universe
would settle, this way
or that. How some would burn,
and others find eternal rest.

Look, she loved him and he died.
So, inscribing his tombstone
in bad Latin
while the great Empire crumbled around her,
she reached out
with one impossible gesture,
and commended him to the mercy
of both Jesus Christ
and the Fates.

Children of Divorce

"We should imagine that we are in heaven,"
I read, as the pilot announces a holding pattern.
Two children of divorce
are busy with the game of "Doorbell."
"Who's there?"
they shout, every time
a bell sounds; they pretend to look for faces
in the storm clouds. The attendant has seated them together,
a boy and a girl,

pretending not to be afraid.
"We should imagine that we are in heaven,"
insists Theodore of Mopsuestia, a name
the children would adore, no doubt
a close relation of Mopsy
Cottontail. The world robes itself
in ribbons of light, each inundated place on earth
a shiny coin, a medium of exchange
in the brooding dark through which we pass.
The girl asks: "Can a tornado pick up a plane and throw it?"
The boy says, "I can't look, it's too scary,"

as he pulls down the window shade.
"It's an ocean down there," says the girl,
"we'll be lost at sea."
"It's too scary," the boy says again,
lifting the shade
as the pilot announces our approach for landing
in Minneapolis. Theodore
and the girl are right:
it doesn't look like any world we know.

"We're gonna die," says the girl.
"I can't look," says the boy, "we're not gonna make it."
"Oh—is that the city—aren't the lights pretty?"
"We're not gonna make it."
The great river shines in the newly minted dusk—pale
and black, red, white—"He'll never make the runway,"
the boy exclaims, "We're gonna die." "Oh,"
says the girl,
"just look at the lights."

Afterward,

the soldiers argued: did she prove
that God exists?

The corpse of a girl, thirteen at most,
lies bloodied on a hill
named for the cross of Jesus Christ,
nothing left
of her voice crying out,
small as a bird,
singing hymns as they raped her,
one long afternoon, the others
already dead,
twenty-three children bayoneted,
left to burn, the old hacked
and shot, fallen in the dust
of the village square
of El Mozote.

God speaks like fire,
God's words
are a sword. The soldiers
are stunned, too sated with death
to move. When one finally shot her,
she kept on singing,
her voice a bit weaker than before.
Another shot, and still she sang
and the soldiers became afraid.
One unsheathed his machete
and hacked through her neck
until at last, the singing stopped.

Afterward,
they argue: does she prove
that God exists? The soldiers are afraid,
and it burns within:
is it fear,
or singing, that has no end?

The Companionable Dark

Friend and neighbor you have taken away,
my one companion is darkness.
—Psalm 88

The companionable dark
of here and now,
seed lying dormant
in the earth. The dark
to which all lost things come—scarves
and rings and precious photographs, and
of course, our beloved
dead. The brooding dark,
our most vulnerable hours, limbs loose
in sleep, mouths agape.
The faithful dark,
where each door leads,
each one of us, alone.
The dark of God come close
as breath, our one companion
all the way through, the dark
of a needle's eye.

Not the easy dark
of dust and candles, but dark
from which comforts flee.
The deep down dark
of one by one,
dark of wind
and dust, dark in which stars burn.
The floodwater dark
of hope, Jesus in agony
in the garden, Esther pacing
her bitter palace. A dark
by which we see, dark like truth,

like flesh on bone:
Help me, who am alone,
and have no help but thee.

What Song, Then?

By the rivers of Babylon
there we sat and wept . . .
—Psalm 137

When my life is alien soil
and a wind
like fear
makes restless ground
of all I've done—

what song, then,
to send out roots
to drink the rain
that does not come—

how could I sing?

Watch light come
from dark and mist rise
from waters; sky and shore
emerge out of night,
and a tree half-green,
half-bare.

Half-afraid of what is in me
(though God has called it good)
I sob over nothing,

desires I cannot name.

Sing us, they say,
a song you remember . . .

Goodness

Despite our good deeds,
the chatter
of our best intentions,
our many kindnesses,
God is at work
in us, close
to the bone,
past the sinews
of our virtues, to the marrow
we cannot feel,
the sudden, helpless tears
when we know what we are,
and can go on.

Naming the Living God

"The Special Theory came to me,"
Einstein said,
"as shifting forms of light."
Riemann once remarked, "I did not
invent those pairs of differential equations. I found them
in the world,
where God had hidden them."

Natural numbers stand firm,
granite laced
with ice.
Negative numbers roam, lions
about to pounce.

All things change
when you measure them. You might as well
sing, the sound of your voice
joining the others, like waters overflowing,
the name of the living God.

Emily in Choir

Emily holds her father's hand,
she dances in place
through the Invitatory
and refuses the book with no pictures.
"This is boring," she whispers,
in the silence between psalms.

Candles lit in honor of the guardian angels
make rivers of air that bend the stone
walls of the abbey church. "Why are the men
wearing costumes?" Emily asks.
"They're the brothers," her father
explains, and Emily says, "Well!
They must have a very strict mother!"

The Grave is strict, says another Emily;
Emily here and now plays with the three
shadows her hands make
on the open page. *While the clergyman
tells Father and Vinnie that "this Corruptible
shall put on Incorruption," it has already done so
and they go defrauded.*

Brimful of knowledge, Emily shakes my arm:
"They're the monks!" she says,
"The men who sing," and she runs
up the aisle, out into the day,

to where the angels are:
*In the name of the Bee—
And of the Butterfly—
And of the Breeze—Amen!*

The Tolling

Walking uphill
in the great womb of dawn,
words of Thérèse come to me,
. . . *my little story, which was like a fairy tale,*
has turned into prayer. And people must
have puddings, Emily Dickinson chimes in,
with the same tone of wonder, into
the jumble of my mind.

Climbing the long hill
to church, I wonder
at the coming of the light,
how dusk after vespers
was the same, beyond purple
or blue, a sky
that made me sing.
Easter, 1896: bit by bit,
Thérèse coughed out
her lungs and faith
turned dark, *my faith*
that Dark adores, Emily
whispers, more solemn now.

Orion stands watch
above the bell tower.
I enter and take a seat
in the monk's choir.
"Let us pray for Brother Louis," says the prayer leader,
and after, a monk appears, like an angel
of the resurrection, to show me hymns
Louis wrote—years ago,
now—the poetry clean
and spare—and to tell the story: how the plague
touched his heart, and Louis went to Minneapolis

to care for AIDS patients. How his heart
gave out and he had to come home,
how long he suffered.

Louis's poetry still makes us sing—
the hospice is in others' hands.
Young monks will carry his body into church
through the baptistry, where it all began.
They will bury him up the hill.

I sit out the tolling
in the Mary chapel;
carved eight hundred years ago
by hands of faith,
she sits very still, with my friend Clellie's face,
the face of any mother.
Tears come, not for Louis,
whom I never knew. And it is not
the tolling, insistent as death.
It is not the length of it—how
long will it go on—I have things to do, I'm hungry,
morning goes so fast—
not the tolling,
but the silence after.

Hide and Seek

Your true and only Son is love.
—Louis Blenkner, O.S.B., *Te Deum*

A thunderclap
rakes the field of sleep—must be
the consecration, enough
to wake the dead—lightning
so soon after, Brother John saw it
arc through the church. We
said good-bye to Louis, and rains came
at the Agnus Dei, our need for tears
answered by the elements. I get up
to close the window: Wichita,
3:09 A.M.
by the light
of the alarm clock, a hotel room
facing east. The city skyline
jumps with each bolt, playing
hide and seek.

Hide and seek: Maria
in the baptistry on her second
birthday, running around the granite font;
that night, Louis's coffin
carried in and blessed there.
Hide and seek, the saints
in light, who have died
and live—Louis's
words to me, though we never met—
that helped me live through an evil time.

I know
the grubby strivings
for each syllable, the search for words
that bolt and run. Louis,

I give thanks for you, for
all that drove you to it.
I give thanks
for the way it all goes on,
thunder and lightning,
the message
and the messenger, great
bone-white wings
that part the sky
as we carry you to your grave. For folds of earth
that admit us all—and a crescent
of blue light I never saw—for unsearchable riches
that reach into our lives, love
calling us by name.

La Vierge Romane

Her face long
and plain, impossibly
serene, has prayed
through blood
and water,
childbirth and death,
these eight centuries past.
She has let her hands fall
open, the child secure
on her lap, old
beyond his years.

"There is your son," Jesus says
from the cross—his stretched hands
powerless—"there, your mother."
And here, during Easter,
the two-months infant nurses
beside me, in the monk's choir,
knowing only mother,
the milk
of all promise,
hands kneading greedily
at the breast. The man
in the choir stall before me, whose mother
has just died, holds his hands
behind his back,
as if a prisoner
being led to a fearful place.

I think I will go
where words are neither hard
nor loving,
but blaze unseen in bones
that grieve, in bones that thrive

and grow. And all that binds
the child to mother will be
sweet food, like sun on stone,
on the wood of the Virgin's face.

She prays for us,
but silently. Her hands hold on
by letting go. From her
the child learns
to give us to each other.

The Room

> I went to the Room, as soon as you had gone, to
> confirm your presence. . . .
>
> —Emily Dickinson, in a letter to Samuel Bowles, 1877

Once you had gone,
your absence filled the room,
like changing light,
like song.

You were wherever
I looked, unloseable
friend—river's edge,
wind on water,
leaves all green flame.

Oh, dear Jesus, I am learning to say,
and the face of Christ you left me—"not stern
but sad," you said, "very Russian"—
gazes back at me
with a human face.

I am with you always,
he said,
when all I wanted
was to see you again.

I tasted you
in the bread and wine.

Who Do You Say That I Am?

Morning and evening,
womb before dawn:

nova of blossom,
star in the apple,
word on the wind.

Long thorn of black locust,
ironwood bark, as
warm as skin:

the infant's hand,
unfolding, light
that forms the eye:

the messenger,
the one,
whatever makes us sing:

emergence,
return,
the end of the spectrum,
beginning of light.
Light.

Nutrition

Off-site now,
we deliver hot meals
in a fierce winter. I knock,
and shake my boots,
treading carefully
on ancient linoleum
buckled
on a wounded
hardwood floor.

Valentine roses
have lost their bloom;
wrinkled, they droop
on their stems,
as if weighted
by beauty.

Their beauty. Yes.
Like the widow's icy walk,
her gnarled fingers
on the lap robe
in the musty living room,
the Bible open
to Isaiah 35:
and the desert shall rejoice,
and blossom . . .

her wrinkly smile
as I knock
and enter. Beauty, yes. All of it.
And truth.

The Presbyterian Women Serve Coffee
at the Home

"I'm so afraid," one says,
"of growing old."
"Not of growing old," says another,
"but catastrophic illness."
"Becoming helpless," adds one,
"losing the little mind I've got."
We laugh, and throw out coffee grounds.

"And yet," says one,
"I see my grandmother now,
and remember her as she was.
It's hard for me,
but I wonder
how unhappy she really is."

"They live in the past," says one.
"It's a kind of mercy," says another.
"Their husbands haven't died,
all their children are still young.
They make no distinction
between the living and the dead."

"It must be like eternal life,"
says one who wipes the coffee pot
and folds the dishtowels.

Fear passes out of us.
We scoop up cookie crumbs
and scour out the sink.
Then we each go our own way, unaccountably happy.

Gold of Ophir

My heart overflows with noble words . . .
—Psalm 45

In the dawn, homing
nighthawks pass
a pale sliver of moon
on the rise.

A horse snorts
in the near-dark,
a killdeer keens, a meadlowlark
embellishes the air

and the sun,

thunderous silence,
touches trees and rooftops
with gold.

Barefoot in the morning chill,
my neighbor stands smoking
on her back porch, teenager
with a newborn,
the father in jail.

Bewildered, proud,
dazzled by new passion,
she takes me in
and shows me her daughter,
who sleeps grandly,
like a queen.

Body and Blood

I am worn, spent,
torn with sorrows—
still, I walk
in the blue light of dawn
and the sky upholds me—
a crescent of moon,
a wing of cloud,
deep crimson, ascends
in the east, tinting even the western sky.

Stupid with worry,
worries—and they are legion—
I stop to admire the weedy hollyhocks
by a neighbor's backyard fence.

I hear the bumblebee
before I spot him
entering a blossom,
his body quivering
like an infant's mouth at the breast,
drinking the milk of the world.

Acknowledgments

"Body and Blood" first appeared in *Spirituality & Health*;
"Gold of Ophir," in *Midwest Quarterly;* and "Return of Swamp
Thing," in *Image: A Journal of the Arts & Religion.*

"The Ignominy of the Living" and "Giveaway" originally
appeared in *The New Yorker.*

"Luke 14: A Commentary" was first published in *Cross Currents,*
no. 4 (winter 1994–95).

"The Astronomy of Love," "The Gift of Tears," "Numbers,"
and "The Presbyterian Women Serve Coffee at the Home," first
appeared in *How I Came to Drink My Grandmother's Piano,*
Marvin, S. Dak.: Benet Biscop Press, Blue Cloud Abbey, 1989.

"Goodness," "La Vierge Romane," "Naming the Living God,"
"The Room," and "Who Do You Say That I Am?" first
appeared in *The Astronomy of Love,* New York: Haybarn Press,
1994. Poems by Kathleen Norris, prints by Ed Colker.

"Nutrition" first appeared in *The Quotidian Mysteries,* New York:
Paulist Press, under license by Riverhead Books, 1998.

The psalms (on pages 111, 112, and 127) are from *The Grail
Psalter.* Chicago: GIA Publications.

The Song of Solomon excerpts are from the King James
Version.

The other Bible quotations (on pages 93, 101, 102, and 124)
are from the New Revised Standard Version.

The author would like to express her gratitude to Ben Belitt,
Claude Fredericks, Linda Hogan, and the good people at
Wayland Press, Gregory Orr of the *Virginia Quarterly Review;*
Ed Ochester at Pittsburgh, and Keith Egan of the Spirituality
Center at St. Mary's College, Notre Dame, Indiana. A special
thanks to the artist Ed Colker, whose love of poetry
illuminates the many volumes of verse, including my own,
that he has published over three decades, and to Brother
Benet Tvetden, O.S.B., a support and soul mate to writers on

the Great Plains, for using up his abbey's leftover paper to print my poems.

I am especially grateful for the friendship and mentoring of Elizabeth Kray, who was an ardent and eloquent advocate for several generations of American poets, and for the support I received many years ago from the late Paul Carroll, when he published my first book of poetry.

Photo by Marc Schechter

Kathleen Norris's books of poetry include *The Middle of the World, Little Girls in Church,* and *The Astronomy of Love.* In addition to her best-selling memoirs (all listed as *New York Times* Notable Books), her most recent prose works include *Quotidian Mysteries: Laundry, Liturgy, and "Women's Work." The Virgin of Bennington* (a memoir) and a children's book on Sts. Benedict and Scholastica (in collaboration with the artist Tomie de Paola) are forthcoming. Her honors include grants from the Echoing Green Foundation, the Bush Foundation, the Solomon R. Guggenheim Foundation, and the New York State Council on the Arts. She lives in South Dakota and Honolulu, Hawaii.